DEVELOPER AGENT SECRETS

Everything They Should Have Taught You In Real Estate Class But Didn't

Wisdom Kwati

Copyright © Sept. 2023 by Wisdom Kwati

Ordering Details

To place orders or for details of discounts for bulk purchases by organizations or groups either for support, gift, training packages, fundraising, or any other educational purposes, send an email to wisdomkwati@gmail.com. Visit www.wisdomkwati.com or follow me on @Wisdom Kwati across all social media platforms.

Table of Contents

INTRODUCTION

In the ever-evolving world of real estate, the role of a real estate agent has transformed significantly. There is a need for real estate agents, to navigate their business in a more lucrative and profitable way. This is what this book aims to teach. It goes beyond the traditional teachings of real estate classes, and focuses on the secrets and insights that can make a significant difference in your career as a developer agent.

We will see the essential aspects that can help agents succeed in their profession. From mastering the art of customer service and earning the trust of developers to becoming a local authority in real estate and leveraging modern marketing channels, this book will equip you with the tools and knowledge needed to elevate your business to new heights.

Throughout this book, you will find invaluable insights, practical tips, and insider secrets that can transform your real estate career. It's time to equip yourself with the knowledge and skills necessary to thrive in the industry and maximize your earning potential.

Remember, this book is not a substitute for hard work, dedication, and continuous learning. It is a roadmap to help you navigate the challenges and seize the opportunities that lie ahead. So, let's embark on this journey together, uncovering the developer agent secrets that will propel your real estate business to unprecedented levels of success.

CHAPTER 1

BECOMING A
DEVELOPER AGENT

Tunde Ajayi was a young and ambitious real estate agent with dreams of making a name for himself in the competitive Nigerian developer market. Fresh out of university with a degree in real estate, Tunde believed he had all the knowledge he needed to excel in his chosen field. However, he quickly discovered that the real world was vastly different from what he had learned in the classroom.

As Tunde embarked on his career, he encountered one obstacle after another. He struggled to secure clients and close deals, feeling frustrated and discouraged. It seemed like his peers were effortlessly navigating the developer market, leaving him wondering what he was missing.

Determined to turn his fortunes around, Tunde sought guidance from industry professionals and experienced real estate agents. He realized that his formal education had only provided him with the theoretical knowledge but had failed to equip him with the practical skills needed to succeed in the real estate business.

Just like Tunde, a lot of real estate agents ignore the potentials in becoming a developer agent because they lack practical knowledge of how to navigate that space. A developer agent is a type of real estate agent who specializes in working with property developers. Their main role is to help developers sell the properties they have built or are currently constructing. They act as a bridge between the developers and potential buyers, assisting in the marketing, promotion, and sale of these properties.

Developer agents have a deep understanding of the real estate market, particularly in the area where they operate. They stay updated on market trends, property values, and new development projects happening in the region. This knowledge allows them to provide accurate information and guidance to buyers interested in purchasing properties from developers.

One of the key tasks of a developer agent is to build relationships with builders and developers. By establishing connections in the industry, they gain access to information about new and upcoming projects, exclusive listings, and potential investment opportunities. This helps them provide a wider range of options to their clients.

Developer agents also handle the negotiation and transaction process on behalf of their clients. They negotiate the terms of the sale, the purchase price, and any additional agreements or contingencies. They manage the paperwork and facilitate communication between buyers, sellers, and other parties involved in the transaction.

As a real estate agent operating in the developer market, you play a crucial role in facilitating the buying and selling of properties developed by builders and developers. Your knowledge, expertise, and connections serve as valuable assets in this competitive industry.

Getting Started As A Developer Agent

As a real estate agent operating in the developer market, your main role is to assist buyers and sellers in the process of buying and selling properties that have been developed by builders and developers. To achieve this, you need to pay attention to these:

Knowledge and Expertise: To be successful in this field, it's important to have a deep understanding of the real estate market, especially in the area where you operate. You should stay updated on current market trends, property values, and the development projects happening in the region. This knowledge will help you provide accurate information and guidance to your clients.

Building Relationships: Developing strong relationships with builders and developers is essential. By establishing connections in the industry, you can gain access to information about new and upcoming projects, exclusive listings, and potential investment opportunities. Building trust with developers can also lead to referrals and repeat business.

Marketing and Promotion: As a developer agent, you'll need to effectively market and promote the properties you represent. This involves creating appealing property listings, using various marketing channels (such as online platforms, social media, and print media), and conducting open houses and property tours to attract potential buyers.

Negotiation and Transaction Management: One of your key responsibilities is negotiating on behalf of your clients. This includes negotiating the terms of the sale, the purchase price, and any additional agreements or contingencies. Additionally, you'll need to manage the transaction process, ensuring that all necessary paperwork is completed accurately and facilitating communication between buyers, sellers, and other parties involved.

Client Service and Communication: Providing exceptional customer service is crucial in this industry. You'll need to listen to your clients' needs, respond to their inquiries promptly, and guide them through the buying or selling process. Clear and effective communication is vital to ensure that your clients understand the steps involved and feel supported throughout the transaction.

Continuing Education: Real estate is a dynamic industry, and it's important to stay updated on changes in laws, regulations, and market conditions. Consider pursuing continuing education courses or attending industry events to enhance your knowledge and skills.

Remember, being a developer agent requires hard work, dedication, and the ability to adapt to the ever-changing real estate market. By leveraging your knowledge, expertise, and connections, you can provide valuable assistance to buyers and sellers, and ultimately thrive in the competitive developer market.

Thriving as a Developer Agent

To excel in this niche, you must work with these tips:

Building Relationships: One of the most significant secrets to success as a developer agent lies in building strong relationships with developers. Establishing rapport and trust with reputable builders can give you access to exclusive projects, pre-sales opportunities, and insider information. Maintaining a good working relationship can provide you with a competitive edge in securing prime properties and negotiating favorable terms for your clients.

In-depth Market Research: To be an effective developer agent, you must possess in-depth knowledge of the local real estate market. Stay informed about upcoming projects, trends, pricing, and market demand. Research the developers you work with, including their track record, reputation, and financial stability. This information helps you advise clients and identify lucrative investment opportunities.

Mastering Off-Plan Sales: Developers often offer off-plan sales, where properties are sold before construction or completion. This requires you to be skilled in visualizing architectural plans, understanding building specifications, and effectively conveying the potential of a property to clients. Educating buyers about the benefits and risks associated with off-plan purchases is essential for successful transactions.

Marketing and Promotion: Developer agents must be adept at marketing and promoting both the developer's brand and specific projects. Utilize various channels such as online platforms, social media, email campaigns, and traditional advertising methods to reach potential buyers. Engage in creative marketing strategies to highlight the unique selling points of the properties you represent.

Network Expansion: Building a strong network is crucial in the developer market. Connect with other real estate professionals, investors, lenders, and industry experts. Attend conferences, seminars, and networking events to expand your circle and gain valuable insights. Collaborating with professionals from related fields, such as architects, interior designers, and contractors, can provide you with additional resources and referrals.

The Role of Real Estate Agents in the Developer Market

Real estate agents play a pivotal role in the developer market by bridging the gap between developers and buyers. They act as intermediaries, leveraging their expertise to guide clients through the complex process of purchasing properties developed by builders. Here are some key responsibilities of real estate agents in the developer market:

Market Knowledge: Real estate agents are expected to have a deep understanding of the local market and the nuances of the developer industry. This includes staying updated on market trends, property values, upcoming projects, and the reputation of developers. Armed with this knowledge, agents can provide valuable advice and insights to clients looking to invest in developer properties.

Property Promotion: Agents are responsible for promoting and marketing developer properties to potential buyers. This involves creating compelling property listings, showcasing the unique features of each project, and organizing property viewings. Agents act as advocates for the developer, aiming to generate interest and attract qualified buyers.

Buyer Representation: Real estate agents act as representatives for buyers interested in purchasing properties from developers. They help clients navigate the complex process of purchasing off-plan properties, explaining the terms and conditions, contract details, and payment plans. Agents negotiate on behalf of their clients to secure the best possible deal and ensure their interests are protected.

Transaction Facilitation: Agents facilitate the transaction process, coordinating with developers, buyers, and other parties involved, such as lenders and attorneys. They ensure all necessary paperwork is completed accurately, deadlines are met, and any issues or concerns are addressed promptly. Agents also assist with due diligence, ensuring that buyers have access to all relevant information about the property and developer.

Challenges Developer Agents Face

Market Volatility: The developer market is subject to market fluctuations and economic conditions. You must be prepared to navigate through periods of market uncertainty, where demand and prices can be unpredictable. Adapting to changing market conditions and adjusting strategies accordingly is essential.

Intense Competition: The developer market is highly competitive, with numerous agents vying for exclusive projects and clients. You must differentiate yourself by showcasing your expertise, track record, and ability to deliver exceptional service. Building a strong personal brand and establishing a solid reputation is crucial in standing out from the competition.

Building Trust: Developing trust with both developers and buyers is a significant challenge for real estate agents in the developer industry. You may be cautious about working with new agents, and buyers may be skeptical of off-plan purchases. You must work diligently to build credibility and demonstrate your knowledge and integrity to earn the trust of all parties involved.

Project Risks and Delays: Off-plan purchases carry inherent risks, such as construction delays, changes in project specifications, or even project cancellations. You must educate buyers about these risks and guide them in making informed decisions. Handling such challenges requires effective communication and negotiation skills to manage expectations and resolve issues.

Opportunities For Developer Agents

Lucrative Commissions: The developer market can offer higher commissions compared to traditional real estate transactions. Successful agents who secure exclusive projects and bring in high-value clients can earn substantial rewards. Capitalizing on these opportunities requires a proactive approach to building relationships with developers and consistently delivering results.

Exclusive Access to Projects: Real estate agents operating in the developer market often gain access to exclusive projects and pre-sales opportunities. This provides them with a unique selling proposition and allows them to offer clients access to desirable properties before they hit the general market. When you leverage these opportunities, you can attract motivated buyers seeking early access and potentially secure favorable deals.

Long-Term Relationships: Developing strong relationships with developers can lead to long-term partnerships and a steady flow of business. As developers embark on new projects, they may prefer working with trusted agents who have a proven track record. When you nurture these relationships, you can establish yourself as a go-to professional in the developer market.

Market Expertise and Specialization: Real estate agents who specialize in the developer market can position themselves as experts in this niche. Specialization allows you to deepen your knowledge, stay up-to-date with market trends, and provide superior service to your clients. By becoming the go-to agent for developer properties, you can attract a loyal client base and referrals.

Recognizing The Dynamic Market

In a dynamic market like the developer industry, continuous learning and adaptation are critical for real estate agents to stay competitive. Here's why:

Keeping Up with Market Trends: The developer market is ever-evolving, with new construction techniques, design trends, and buyer preferences emerging regularly. You must stay informed about these trends to advise clients effectively and offer properties that align with current market demands.

Embracing Technological Advancements: Technology plays a significant role in the real estate industry, and the developer market is no exception. You must embrace and leverage technology tools such as virtual tours, 3D modeling, and online marketing platforms to enhance your marketing strategies and provide a seamless buying experience for clients.

Evolving Buyer Expectations: Buyer expectations in the developer market are constantly evolving. Clients seek agents who can offer personalized service, expert guidance, and access to a wide range of information. Agents must adapt their communication styles, marketing approaches, and customer service to meet these changing expectations.

Enhancing Negotiation and Contract Skills: Negotiation skills are paramount in the developer market, as agents often negotiate on behalf of clients for favorable terms and pricing. It is essential for you to continuously enhance your negotiation skills to secure the best deals for your clients. Also, you should stay updated on contract laws, regulations, and clauses specific to the developer market to ensure smooth and legally sound transactions.

Expanding Professional Network: The developer market thrives on strong professional networks. You should actively participate in industry events, conferences, and networking opportunities to expand your connections. Collaborating with professionals from related fields, such as architects, contractors, and lenders, can provide valuable insights and resources, enabling you to offer comprehensive services to your clients.

Continuous Education and Training: A dynamic market demands continuous education and training. Agents should seek opportunities to enhance your knowledge through workshops, seminars, online courses, and certifications. Staying well-informed about industry trends, best practices, and legal requirements allows you to provide up-to-date and accurate advice to your clients.

Adaptability to Changing Market Conditions: The developer market is susceptible to changes in the economy, regulations, and buyer preferences. You must remain adaptable and agile in response to these changes. You should be proactive in adjusting your strategies, marketing approaches, and client engagement techniques to align with shifting market dynamics

In the next chapter, we will look at attracting and retaining the right clients as a developer agent.

CHAPTER 2

ATTRACTING AND RETAINING THE RIGHT CLIENTS

In his quest for knowledge, Tunde was introduced to Mr. Olu, a seasoned developer agent with decades of experience in the industry. Recognizing Tunde's determination and potential, Mr. Olu took him under his wing and became his mentor.

Under Mr. Olu's guidance, Tunde learned that building strong customer relationships was the foundation of success in the developer market. He discovered the importance of effective communication, active listening, and empathy when dealing with clients. Tunde realized that exceptional customer service was not just a buzzword but a genuine way to differentiate himself from the competition and gain the trust of both developers and clients.

Mr. Olu also emphasized the significance of understanding the needs and goals of developers. He taught Tunde negotiation techniques that empowered him to secure favorable terms and conditions for his clients. Tunde learned to approach each negotiation with a win-win mindset, seeking mutually beneficial outcomes for all parties involved.

Building strong customer relationships is crucial in the developer market as it fosters trust, loyalty, and long-term success. As a real estate agent, understanding the needs and expectations of your developer clients is essential for establishing a solid foundation. Let's explore effective strategies for building customer relationships in the developer industry.

To build strong customer relationships with developers, it's important to have a clear understanding of their needs and expectations. Developers often seek agents who can deliver results, provide market insights, and contribute to their overall success. Take the time to understand their project goals, target audience, desired timelines, and financial considerations. By aligning your services with their specific requirements, you position yourself as a valuable partner.

Effective communication is crucial when it comes to establishing trust and building a strong relationship with your developer clients. It serves as the foundation for successful collaboration and understanding. Here are some strategies that can help you communicate effectively:

a. Active Listening: Listening actively means giving your full attention to developers' concerns, ideas, and visions for their projects. It involves showing genuine interest by asking relevant questions and seeking a deeper understanding of their objectives. By actively listening, you demonstrate respect and validate their perspective, fostering a sense of trust and rapport.

b. Transparent and Timely Updates: Keeping developers well-informed is essential. This involves sharing updates about market trends, property developments, and sales progress in a transparent and timely manner. Providing detailed reports, market analyses, and feedback from potential buyers helps them make informed decisions. Transparent communication builds trust and confidence, as developers appreciate being kept in the loop.

c. Professionalism and Reliability: Demonstrating professionalism in all interactions is vital. This means being punctual, responsive, and reliable. Developers value agents who can be trusted to fulfill their commitments consistently. By maintaining a professional demeanor, you convey reliability and competence, which enhances their confidence in your abilities.

d. Customized Communication Channels: Understanding the preferred communication channels of your developer clients is key. Some may prefer face-to-face meetings for more personalized discussions, while others may favor email or phone conversations for convenience. By adapting your communication style to their preferences, you ensure effective and comfortable interactions. This flexibility shows your willingness to accommodate their needs and preferences, fostering a positive working relationship.

Employing these strategies will help you create an environment of effective communication that promotes trust, understanding, and successful collaboration with your developer clients.

Standing Out from Your Competitors

To stand out from your competitors in the competitive developer market, it's essential to provide exceptional customer service that goes above and beyond. Here are some strategies to help you deliver outstanding service:

a. Personalized Attention: Treat each developer client as a top priority by taking the time to understand their unique needs and goals. Tailor your services and advice to align with their specific requirements. By providing personalized attention, you demonstrate that you value their business and are committed to helping them achieve their objectives.

b. Attention to Detail: Pay close attention to every detail throughout the buying and selling process. Anticipate potential challenges or issues and address them proactively to ensure a smooth and hassle-free transaction experience. When you are thorough and meticulous, you instill confidence in your clients and show that you are dedicated to delivering a high level of service.

c. Proactive Market Insights: Stay up-to-date with market trends, competitor analysis, and buyer preferences. Share valuable, data-driven insights with your developer clients, providing them with a competitive edge. By keeping them informed about market dynamics and opportunities, you position yourself as a trusted advisor and help them make informed decisions that align with their business objectives.

d. Value-Added Services: Offer additional services that go beyond traditional real estate transactions. For example, connect your developer clients with trusted professionals such as architects, contractors, or interior designers who can assist with their projects. By providing access to a comprehensive network of resources, you add value and enhance the overall customer experience. This demonstrates your commitment to supporting their success beyond the basic scope of your services.

This way, you can differentiate yourself from competitors and establish a reputation for exceptional customer service in the developer market. Building strong relationships, providing personalized attention, and delivering added value will help you attract and retain satisfied clients.

Activating Repeat Business

To activate repeat business and foster long-term relationships with developers, it's important to nurture these connections and position yourself as a trusted partner. Here are some strategies to help you achieve this:

a. Consistent Follow-up: Maintain regular communication with developers even after completing a project. Follow up to ensure their satisfaction, address any concerns, and express your interest in their future projects. By staying in touch and demonstrating your commitment to their success, you can strengthen the relationship and increase the likelihood of repeat business.

b. Networking and Referrals: Actively engage in networking activities within the developer community. Attend industry events, join relevant associations, and participate in forums where developers gather. By expanding your network and building relationships with developers, you not only increase your visibility but also enhance your chances of receiving referrals and accessing new opportunities.

c. Stay Updated and Offer Value: Stay informed about the market trends, industry news, and regulatory changes that may impact developers' projects. Share valuable insights, reports, and information with them regularly. By positioning yourself as a knowledgeable resource, you demonstrate your expertise and dedication to providing value beyond transactional services.

d. Be a Trusted Advisor: Strive to be a trusted advisor to developers by offering guidance, market expertise, and strategic advice. Take the time to understand their goals and challenges, and provide customized solutions that align with their objectives. By offering your insights and expertise, you become a valuable resource and partner in their decision-making process.

You can cultivate long-lasting relationships with developers, activate repeat business, and position yourself as a trusted advisor in the industry. Building trust, offering value, and maintaining open lines of communication will help you establish a strong foundation for ongoing collaboration and mutual success.

Remember, building strong customer relationships in the developer market takes time and effort. It's important to invest in the long-term success of your relationships with developers. Here are additional strategies to nurture and strengthen those relationships:

Personalized Engagement: Take a personalized approach to engagement with developers. Remember their preferences, project details, and specific requirements. This level of attention shows your commitment and builds trust. Send personalized messages, greetings, and updates to maintain a personal connection.

Collaboration and Partnership: Position yourself as a partner rather than just a service provider. Collaborate with developers on various aspects of their projects, such as marketing strategies, target audience analysis, and pricing recommendations. Offer your expertise and insights to help them make informed decisions. This collaborative approach fosters a sense of mutual respect and strengthens the relationship.

Continued Support: Provide ongoing support even after the completion of a project. Offer assistance with post-sales services, such as coordinating with buyers for unit handovers or resolving any post-purchase issues. When you go the extra mile to ensure a smooth transition and customer satisfaction, you demonstrate your commitment to long-term success.

Celebrate Successes: Celebrate milestones and successes with developers. Recognize their achievements and contributions in the market. This can include congratulatory messages, acknowledgments in marketing materials, or joint marketing initiatives to promote their projects. Celebrating successes together reinforces the positive relationship and encourages future collaboration.

Seek Feedback: Regularly seek feedback from developers about their experience working with you. Ask for suggestions on how you can improve your services or provide additional value. Act on the feedback received to continuously enhance your offerings and address any areas of improvement. This proactive approach demonstrates your commitment to meeting their needs.

Loyalty Programs and Incentives: Consider implementing loyalty programs or incentives for developers who engage in multiple projects with you. Offer exclusive benefits such as priority access to listings, reduced commission rates, or additional marketing exposure. These incentives incentivize developers to continue working with you and reinforce their loyalty.

Industry Knowledge Sharing: Share industry knowledge, market reports, and relevant articles with developers. Keep them updated on emerging trends, regulatory changes, and market insights. Providing valuable information showcases your expertise and reinforces your position as a trusted advisor.

Remember, building strong customer relationships is an ongoing process. Continuously invest in nurturing and strengthening these relationships to foster loyalty, generate referrals, and secure repeat business. By consistently delivering exceptional service, demonstrating value, and maintaining open lines of communication, you can become a trusted partner for developers in the long run.

CHAPTER 3

COLLABORATING WITH DEVELOPERS

As Tunde's knowledge and confidence grew, Mr. Olu opened the doors to the mysterious world of developers. Tunde attended industry events, networked with key players, and immersed himself in the dynamic landscape of development projects. He quickly realized that working with developers required a collaborative approach based on trust and understanding.

Tunde learned to navigate the complexities of development projects, from understanding the intricacies of zoning regulations to assessing the feasibility of a project. He discovered the importance of conducting thorough due diligence on developers and their previous projects, ensuring they had a solid track record of delivering quality work.

With Mr. Olu's guidance, Tunde honed his skills in assessing the market potential of development projects. He learned to identify emerging trends and to recognize the indicators of a successful project. Tunde realized that by providing accurate market insights to developers, he could position himself as a valuable asset and trusted advisor.

Amidst his journey, Tunde encountered a charismatic developer who promised sky-high returns on a project. Initially enticed by the opportunity, Tunde's intuition and Mr. Olu's teachings urged him to exercise caution. He delved into thorough due diligence, investigating the developer's track record and past projects.

To Tunde's dismay, his investigations revealed a trail of fraudulent schemes and disappointed investors. He discovered that the developer had a history of deceiving clients and failing to deliver on promises. Armed with this knowledge, Tunde took a stand against deceit and fraud in the industry.

Determined to protect his clients and maintain his integrity, Tunde became an advocate for transparency and authenticity. He educated his clients about the warning signs of fraudulent schemes and the importance of conducting thorough research before investing. Tunde made it his mission to ensure that his clients were well-informed and invested in genuine offers. He also ensures that property agents under him were armed with the right information.

Working with developers in a collaborative manner is essential for establishing a mutually beneficial relationship. As a real estate agent, adopting a collaborative approach allows you to build trust, earn the confidence of developers, negotiate favorable terms, and understand their perspective and motivations. Let's explore these aspects in detail:

Developing a Mutually Beneficial Relationship with Developers

To foster a mutually beneficial relationship with developers, it's important to demonstrate your commitment to their success. Here are strategies to consider:

a. Open and Transparent Communication: Maintain clear and open lines of communication with developers. Keep them informed about market trends, buyer feedback, and the progress of sales.

Share updates regularly, addressing any concerns promptly. This transparency helps build trust and ensures that both parties are on the same page.

b. Collaborative Planning: Engage in collaborative planning with developers to align your strategies with their project goals. Discuss target audience profiles, pricing strategies, and marketing approaches together. By involving them in the decision-making process, you demonstrate that their input is valued, which strengthens the relationship.

c. Understanding Project Vision: Invest time in understanding the developer's vision for the project. Discuss their objectives, target market, and unique selling points. By aligning your efforts with their vision, you can better market the property and attract the right buyers.

Strategies for Earning Developers' Trust and Confidence

Building trust and earning the confidence of developers is crucial. Here are strategies to establish yourself as a trustworthy and reliable partner:

a. Expertise and Market Knowledge: Demonstrate your expertise and deep understanding of the local real estate market. Showcase your track record of successful sales and your knowledge of the developer industry. By positioning yourself as an industry expert, you instill confidence in developers that you can effectively market their projects.

b. Consistent Performance: Consistently deliver results and exceed expectations. This includes achieving sales targets, providing accurate market analysis, and offering exceptional customer service. Your consistent performance builds trust and confidence in your abilities.

c. Honesty and Integrity: Maintain the highest level of honesty and integrity in all your dealings with developers. Avoid exaggerations or false promises. Be transparent about challenges and risks, and provide realistic expectations. Your ethical approach fosters trust and establishes a solid foundation for the relationship.

Negotiation Techniques for Favorable Terms and Conditions

Negotiation is a critical aspect of working with developers. Here are techniques to employ during negotiations:

a. Preparedness: Before entering negotiations, thoroughly research the market, comparable properties, and the developer's motivations. Understand their desired outcomes and constraints. Armed with this information, you can present well-informed arguments and negotiate effectively.

b. Win-Win Solutions: Aim for win-win solutions where both parties benefit. Look for creative alternatives that address the developer's concerns while protecting your clients' interests. By demonstrating a willingness to find mutually beneficial outcomes, you build trust and foster a positive negotiation environment.

c. Assertiveness and Persuasion: Be assertive in representing your clients' interests while remaining respectful and professional. Use persuasive communication techniques to articulate your arguments and present compelling evidence or data to support your position. Effective persuasion helps in achieving favorable terms and conditions for your clients.

Understanding the Developer's Perspective and Motivations

To work effectively with developers, it's crucial to understand their perspective and motivations. Consider the following:

a. Profitability and ROI: Developers are primarily motivated by profitability and return on investment. Understand their financial goals and the factors that impact their profitability, such as construction costs, market demand, and pricing strategies. Align your efforts with their goals to establish a mutually beneficial partnership.

b. Time Constraints: Developers often work within tight timelines to complete projects and start generating revenue. Appreciate the importance of timely sales and the need to adhere to project schedules. Prioritize your activities and provide efficient support to help developers meet their deadlines.

c. Market Competition: Developers operate in a competitive market where differentiation is key. Understand the competitive landscape and how your marketing strategies can effectively position their projects. Provide insights on market trends, buyer preferences, and innovative approaches to stand out from competitors.

d. Risk Management: Developers face various risks throughout the development process, such as financial risks, regulatory compliance, and market fluctuations. By understanding their risk profile and concerns, you can offer guidance and support in mitigating risks. This proactive approach demonstrates your commitment to their success and builds trust.

e. Long-Term Vision: Developers often have a long-term vision for their business, including multiple projects and growth plans. Take the time to understand their broader goals and align your services to support their vision. By demonstrating your understanding of their aspirations, you become a trusted partner for their future endeavors.

In conclusion, working with developers in a collaborative manner involves developing a mutually beneficial relationship based on trust, confidence, and understanding. By adopting effective communication strategies, demonstrating expertise and integrity, employing negotiation techniques, and understanding the developer's perspective and motivations, you can establish yourself as a valued partner. This collaborative approach not only strengthens your relationship with developers but also enhances your ability to deliver exceptional results and seize opportunities in the dynamic developer market.

CHAPTER 4

BECOMING THE AUTHORITY IN YOUR INDUSTRY

As Tunde continued to establish himself in the developer market, he recognized the importance of positioning himself as an authority in real estate within his domain. He understood that becoming a trusted source of knowledge and information would not only attract clients but also solidify his reputation as a reliable and knowledgeable agent.

Tunde began by immersing himself in the local real estate landscape. He studied the market trends, tracked property values, and familiarized himself with the unique features and attractions of different neighborhoods. By understanding the intricacies of the local market, Tunde was able to provide his clients with valuable insights and guidance specific to their needs.

To showcase his expertise, Tunde started writing informative articles and blog posts about the local real estate market. He shared his insights on property investment, market trends, and tips for buyers and sellers. His content was well-researched and focused on providing actionable advice to his audience.

Tunde also embraced public speaking opportunities. He volunteered to give presentations at local community events, homeowner associations, and business organizations. By sharing his knowledge and experiences, Tunde established himself as a trusted authority in the real estate field, further enhancing his reputation.

To expand his reach, Tunde explored various media channels. He reached out to local newspapers, radio stations, and online platforms to offer his expertise as a guest contributor or interviewee. His goal was to provide valuable information to a wider audience and increase his visibility as a go-to resource for real estate-related matters.

In addition to traditional media, Tunde recognized the power of social media in amplifying his message and connecting with potential clients. He created profiles on popular social networking platforms and developed a content strategy that resonated with his target audience. Tunde regularly shared market updates, success stories, and practical advice, engaging with his followers and building a community around his brand.

As Tunde's reputation as an authority grew, he began receiving invitations to participate in panel discussions and industry conferences. He seized these opportunities to share his knowledge and engage in meaningful conversations with other experts in the field. These collaborations not only expanded his network but also further solidified his position as a respected figure in the real estate industry.

By positioning himself as an authority, Tunde gained the trust and respect of both clients and industry peers. His expertise became sought-after, and clients sought his guidance in making informed decisions about their real estate investments. Tunde's commitment to being a reliable source of information propelled his career to new heights, establishing him as a leading developer agent in Nigeria.

With each chapter of his journey, Tunde grew more confident in his abilities and gained a deeper understanding of the secrets to success in the developer market. Through the lessons he learned and the challenges he overcame, Tunde transformed from a novice agent into a respected figure in the real estate industry. His unwavering commitment to exceptional customer service, transparency, and continuous learning became the pillars of his thriving real estate agency—the Landmark Agent.

Becoming an authority in real estate is a powerful way to establish your expertise, credibility, and influence in a specific market segment. As a real estate agent, positioning yourself as a trusted advisor and resource for developers requires a strategic approach. Let's explore strategies for gaining local knowledge, insights, and leveraging networking opportunities to become a respected local authority.

Establishing Expertise and Credibility in a Specific Market Segment

To become an authority, focus on a specific market segment that aligns with your interests, strengths, and market opportunities. By specializing in a particular property type, such as residential, commercial, or industrial, you can develop a deep understanding of that segment and position yourself as an expert. Consider the following strategies:

a. Market Research and Analysis: Conduct thorough market research to gain insights into the specific market segment. Analyze market trends, supply and demand dynamics, pricing patterns, and investment opportunities. Develop expertise in market analytics and regularly share your findings with developers to showcase your in-depth knowledge.

b. Track Record and Success Stories: Highlight your track record of successful transactions in the chosen market segment. Showcase case studies and success stories that demonstrate your ability to deliver results. Developers are more likely to trust an agent with a proven track record in their specific niche.

c. Continuing Education: Stay updated with industry trends, regulations, and best practices through continuous education and professional development. Attend seminars, workshops, and courses specific to your market segment. Earning certifications or designations in that area further enhances your credibility and expertise.

Strategies for Gaining Local Knowledge and Insights

Developing a deep understanding of the local market is essential to becoming a local authority. Here are strategies to gain local knowledge and insights:

a. Immersion in the Community: Immerse yourself in the local community by actively participating in local events, joining community organizations, and attending neighborhood meetings. This helps you understand the unique characteristics, trends, and challenges of the area.

b. Establish Local Partnerships: Build relationships with local professionals, such as appraisers, architects, contractors, and property managers. Collaborating with these experts provides you with valuable insights and strengthens your network. Share your knowledge and resources with them as well, fostering a mutually beneficial relationship.

c. Monitor Local Media and Publications: Stay informed about local real estate news, developments, and market trends through local newspapers, magazines, online publications, and industry-specific forums. Subscribe to relevant newsletters and follow influential figures in the local real estate scene to stay updated.

d. Attend Local Real Estate Events: Participate in local real estate conferences, seminars, and networking events. These gatherings provide opportunities to connect with industry leaders, developers, and other professionals. Engage in discussions, share your expertise, and learn from others' experiences.

Positioning Yourself as a Trusted Advisor

To position yourself as a trusted advisor and resource for developers, focus on building strong relationships and providing value-added services. Consider the following strategies:

a. Proactive Market Insights: Regularly share market insights, reports, and data-driven analyses with developers. Offer them a comprehensive understanding of the market, including trends, investment potential, and buyer preferences. By providing valuable information, you establish yourself as a knowledgeable resource.

b. Strategic Advisory Services: Offer strategic advice to developers based on your expertise and market knowledge. Assist them in making informed decisions regarding property acquisitions, pricing strategies, market positioning, and risk management. Your guidance demonstrates your commitment to their success and builds trust.

c. Network of Trusted Professionals: Develop a network of trusted professionals, such as architects, contractors, attorneys, and lenders. By connecting developers with reliable resources, you become a valuable asset in their real estate endeavors. This network adds credibility and expands your sphere of influence.

d. Exceptional Customer Service and Support: Provide exceptional customer service and support to developers throughout their projects. Be responsive, proactive, and attentive to their needs. Offer assistance with paperwork, permits, marketing materials, and any other support they may require.

By delivering a high level of service, you reinforce your role as a trusted advisor and resource.

Leveraging Networking Opportunities to Expand Your Influence

Networking is a powerful tool for expanding your influence and becoming a local authority in real estate. Here are strategies to maximize networking opportunities:

a. Industry Associations and Groups: Join local real estate associations, chambers of commerce, and industry-specific groups. Attend their events, participate in committees, and actively engage with fellow members. Networking within these organizations helps you build relationships with influential professionals and developers in your target market.

b. Social Media Presence: Establish a strong presence on social media platforms, particularly those popular among real estate professionals and developers. Share valuable content, market updates, success stories, and industry insights. Engage with your audience by responding to comments and initiating discussions. Social media allows you to reach a broader audience and connect with potential clients and partners.

c. Hosting Events and Workshops: Organize educational events, workshops, or webinars targeting developers and investors. Offer valuable insights, expert speakers, and networking opportunities. By hosting such events, you position yourself as a thought leader and create a platform for industry professionals to connect and learn from each other.

d. Referrals and Recommendations: Encourage satisfied clients, industry partners, and developers you've worked with to provide referrals and recommendations. Word-of-mouth recommendations carry significant weight and can help you establish credibility and attract new business opportunities.

e. Collaborative Projects: Seek opportunities to collaborate with developers on joint projects or marketing initiatives. This could involve co-hosting open houses, participating in project launches, or developing joint marketing campaigns.

Collaboration strengthens relationships, expands your reach, and further positions you as a trusted partner.

Remember, becoming a local authority in real estate requires consistency, dedication, and a genuine commitment to adding value to developers and the local community. By establishing expertise, gaining local knowledge, positioning yourself as a trusted advisor, and leveraging networking opportunities, you can enhance your reputation, attract high-profile clients, and solidify your position as a respected authority in your market segment.

CHAPTER 5

BUILDING A SOLID BUSINESS STRUCTURE

Recognizing the importance of building a solid business structure, Tunde set out to establish a real estate agency that would serve as the foundation for his success. He knew that having efficient operational systems and processes in place was crucial for sustainable growth and customer satisfaction.

Tunde gathered a team of talented individuals who shared his vision and values. He sought out professionals who had expertise in various aspects of the real estate industry, including sales, marketing, finance, and legal affairs. Each team member brought unique skills to the table, and together, they formed a cohesive unit that was committed to delivering exceptional service.

With his team in place, Tunde set about creating a harmonious work environment that fostered professionalism, collaboration, and innovation. He organized regular team meetings to ensure everyone was aligned with the agency's goals and to provide a platform for sharing ideas and insights.

One of the first steps Tunde took was to define clear roles and responsibilities for each team member. He wanted to ensure that everyone understood their specific tasks and that there was no overlap or confusion. This clarity allowed for better coordination and improved efficiency within the agency.

Tunde also emphasized the importance of ongoing training and development. He arranged workshops and seminars where team members could enhance their skills and stay updated with industry trends. Tunde encouraged his team to seek professional certifications and further education to broaden their knowledge and expertise.

To streamline their day-to-day operations, Tunde implemented modern technology solutions. They invested in a customer relationship management (CRM) system that allowed them to manage client interactions, track leads, and streamline communication. The CRM system helped them stay organized and provided valuable data for analyzing customer preferences and market trends.

Additionally, Tunde recognized the significance of maintaining strong relationships with other professionals in the industry. He formed partnerships with reputable lawyers, architects, contractors, and property inspectors. These alliances ensured that their clients received comprehensive services and expert advice throughout the entire real estate process.

As the agency grew, Tunde focused on building a culture of exceptional customer service. They implemented a feedback system to gather client reviews and testimonials, enabling them to continuously improve their services. Tunde stressed the importance of going above and beyond for their clients, understanding their unique needs, and providing personalized solutions.

Tunde's agency soon gained a reputation for professionalism, integrity, and customer satisfaction. They developed a loyal client base that appreciated their attention to detail and commitment to excellence. Word of mouth spread, and the agency began receiving referrals from satisfied clients, further fueling their growth.

Building a solid business structure is crucial for the success and growth of your real estate agency. By establishing a strong foundation, developing effective operational systems and processes, hiring a competent team, and implementing smart technologies and tools, you can set your agency up for long-term success. Let's delve into each aspect in detail:

Establishing a Strong Foundation for Your Real Estate Agency

To build a solid business structure, consider the following key components:

a. Mission and Vision: Define a clear mission and vision for your agency. Your mission statement should outline your purpose and values, while your vision statement sets the direction for future growth and success. These guiding principles provide a foundation for decision-making and strategic planning.

b. Legal Structure and Compliance: Determine the appropriate legal structure for your agency, such as a sole proprietorship, partnership, or limited liability company (LLC). Ensure compliance with local laws, licensing requirements, and professional regulations. Consult legal professionals and accountants to establish a solid legal framework.

c. Financial Management: Implement robust financial management systems to track income, expenses, and profitability. Establish proper bookkeeping practices, budgeting processes, and financial controls. Regularly review financial statements to make informed decisions and ensure financial stability.

Developing Effective Operational Systems and Processes

Efficient operational systems and processes are essential for streamlining your agency's workflow and maximizing productivity. Consider the following strategies:

a. Client Relationship Management (CRM): Implement a reliable CRM system to manage client data, track interactions, and automate communication. This enables you to stay organized, maintain strong client relationships, and leverage data for targeted marketing and sales efforts.

b. Document Management: Establish a centralized document management system to store and organize essential paperwork, contracts, and transaction records. This ensures easy access, reduces administrative burdens, and facilitates compliance with regulatory requirements.

c. Workflow Automation: Identify repetitive tasks and automate them using technology tools or software solutions. This saves time, minimizes errors, and improves overall efficiency. Examples include automated email campaigns, digital signatures, and transaction management systems.

d. Standard Operating Procedures (SOPs): Develop clear SOPs for various aspects of your agency's operations, such as lead generation, client onboarding, marketing, and transaction coordination. SOPs ensure consistency, improve training processes, and enable scalability as your agency grows.

Hiring and Training a Competent Team to Support Your Growth

As your agency expands, hiring and training a competent team is essential for delivering exceptional service and driving growth. Consider the following strategies:

a. Define Roles and Responsibilities: Clearly define roles and responsibilities for each team member based on their expertise and strengths. This promotes efficiency, avoids duplication of efforts, and ensures clarity in job expectations.

b. Recruitment and Selection: Develop a structured recruitment process to attract top talent. Clearly define job requirements, conduct thorough interviews, and consider using skill assessments or tests. Hire individuals who align with your agency's values and goals.

c. Comprehensive Training Programs: Implement comprehensive training programs to onboard new team members and continuously develop their skills. Provide ongoing training on industry trends, sales techniques, negotiation strategies, and customer service. This investment in training enhances team performance and ensures consistent service quality.

d. Foster a Positive Work Culture: Create a positive work environment that promotes collaboration, professional growth, and open communication. Encourage teamwork, recognize achievements, and provide opportunities for professional development. A positive work culture fosters loyalty, productivity, and team synergy.

Implementing Smart Technologies and Tools for Efficiency

Leveraging technology and smart tools can significantly improve the efficiency and effectiveness of your agency's operations. Consider the following:

a. Real Estate Software: Invest in real estate-specific software solutions that automate processes, such as CRM, transaction management, lead generation, and marketing automation. These tools streamline operations, improve data management, and enhance client communication.

b. Online Marketing and Lead Generation: Utilize digital marketing strategies and online platforms to generate leads and expand your agency's reach. Implement search engine optimization (SEO) techniques, social media marketing, and email marketing campaigns. Leverage lead generation tools and analytics to track and optimize your marketing efforts.

c. Virtual and Remote Tools: Embrace virtual and remote technologies to facilitate communication and collaboration with clients and team members. Utilize video conferencing platforms, project management tools, and virtual tour software to conduct meetings, showcase properties, and manage projects efficiently.

d. Mobile Apps and Communication Tools: Equip your team with mobile apps and communication tools that enable real-time collaboration, task management, and instant communication. This ensures smooth coordination and responsiveness in a fast-paced industry.

e. Data Analytics and Market Intelligence: Leverage data analytics tools to gain insights into market trends, buyer preferences, and performance metrics. Analyze data to make data-driven decisions, identify growth opportunities, and stay ahead of the competition.

When you implement smart technologies and tools, you can streamline operations, improve efficiency, and enhance the overall client experience. You can position your agency for long-term success, ensure smooth operations, deliver exceptional service, and stay ahead in a competitive market. Continuously assess and adapt your business structure to meet the evolving needs of your agency and the real estate industry as a whole.

CHAPTER 6

BECOME A DIGITAL FRONTIER

Tunde recognized the immense potential of digital marketing and social media in expanding their reach and connecting with a wider audience. He understood that in today's digital age, having a strong online presence was crucial for business success. Tunde decided to invest in a comprehensive digital marketing strategy to elevate their brand and attract more clients.

They revamped their website to make it more user-friendly, visually appealing, and informative. The website became a hub of valuable content, featuring blog articles, market insights, and guides for buyers and sellers. Tunde understood the importance of providing valuable resources to their target audience to establish their agency as a trusted authority in the real estate industry.

Tunde and his team also developed a strong presence on social media platforms. They created engaging content that showcased their expertise, market knowledge, and success stories. They shared informative videos, conducted live Q&A sessions, and collaborated with influencers to expand their reach.

To further enhance their online visibility, Tunde invested in targeted online advertising campaigns. They utilized social media ads, search engine marketing, and email marketing to reach potential clients who were actively looking to buy or sell properties. They focused on targeting specific demographics and geographic areas to ensure their marketing efforts were highly effective.

Tunde also recognized the power of personal branding in the digital space. He understood that establishing himself as a trusted and recognizable figure would not only benefit the agency but also open doors to new opportunities. Tunde dedicated time and effort to develop his personal brand as the face of the agency.

He started by crafting a compelling personal story that resonated with his target audience. Tunde shared his journey, the challenges he overcame, and his unwavering commitment to providing exceptional service. He showcased his expertise through thought-provoking articles, insightful videos, and engaging social media posts.

Tunde leveraged his personal brand to become a sought-after speaker at real estate conferences and industry events. He shared his knowledge and experiences, inspiring aspiring real estate agents to embrace the secrets of success in the developer market. Tunde's dynamic and engaging presentations captivated the audience, establishing him as a thought leader in the industry.

In addition to his personal branding efforts, Tunde encouraged his team members to build their personal brands as well. He recognized that showcasing the expertise and individual strengths of his team would further enhance the agency's reputation and credibility. The team members started sharing their insights and experiences through blog posts, social media content, and guest appearances on industry podcasts.

The agency's digital marketing efforts and strong personal branding strategies paid off. Their online presence flourished, attracting a steady stream of leads and inquiries. Tunde and his team diligently followed up on these leads, nurturing relationships and converting them into loyal clients.

Harnessing the power of marketing and social media is essential for maximizing your impact as a real estate agent. By creating a compelling personal brand, leveraging social media platforms, implementing targeted marketing campaigns, and measuring your efforts, you can effectively reach and engage with your target audience. Let's explore each aspect in detail:

Creating a Compelling Personal Brand for Maximum Impact

    a. Define Your Unique Selling Proposition (USP): Identify what sets you apart from other real estate agents. Determine your unique strengths, expertise, and value proposition. This forms the foundation of your personal brand and helps you differentiate yourself in the market.

b. Craft a Consistent Brand Identity: Develop a cohesive brand identity that aligns with your USP. Design a professional logo, choose a color palette, and create a visually appealing website and marketing materials. Consistency in your branding helps establish recognition and credibility among your target audience.

c. Showcase Your Expertise: Position yourself as an expert in your niche. Create valuable content, such as blog posts, videos, or podcasts, that demonstrate your knowledge and provide helpful insights to your target audience. Share success stories, industry trends, and tips that showcase your expertise and build trust.

d. Develop a Strong Online Presence: Establish a professional and engaging online presence through a well-designed website and active profiles on relevant social media platforms. Your online presence should reflect your brand and serve as a hub for sharing valuable content, property listings, and client testimonials.

Leveraging Social Media Platforms to Reach and Engage with Target Audiences

a. Identify Your Target Audience: Understand the demographics, interests, and behaviors of your target audience. This knowledge enables you to tailor your messaging and select the most appropriate social media platforms to reach them effectively.

b. Choose the Right Social Media Platforms: Select social media platforms that align with your target audience's preferences and demographics. For example, platforms like Facebook, Instagram, LinkedIn, or YouTube may be suitable for different segments of your audience. Focus your efforts on the platforms where your target audience is most active.

c. Create Engaging Content: Develop compelling content that resonates with your target audience. Share visually appealing property photos, virtual tours, informative videos, market updates, and tips related to real estate. Encourage audience interaction through comments, likes, and shares to increase engagement and expand your reach.

d. Engage in Conversations: Actively engage with your audience by responding to comments, direct messages, and inquiries. Foster conversations, answer questions, and provide valuable insights. This engagement builds rapport, trust, and strengthens your relationships with potential clients and industry peers.

Implementing Targeted Marketing Campaigns to Attract Developers and Investors

a. Define Your Target Market: Identify the specific segment of developers and investors you want to target. Determine their unique needs, preferences, and pain points. This allows you to tailor your marketing messages and strategies accordingly.

b. Develop a Strategic Marketing Plan: Create a comprehensive marketing plan that outlines your objectives, target audience, key messages, and channels. Incorporate both online and offline marketing tactics to maximize your reach. Consider strategies like email marketing, content marketing, paid advertising, and partnerships with industry influencers.

c. Highlight Your Value Proposition: Clearly communicate the benefits and value you offer to developers and investors. Showcase your track record, market expertise, and unique insights. Emphasize how partnering with you can help them achieve their goals, whether it's finding profitable investment opportunities or navigating complex development projects.

d. Utilize Data-Driven Marketing: Leverage data and analytics to optimize your marketing campaigns. Track key performance indicators (KPIs), such as website traffic, lead generation, and conversion rates. Analyze the data to identify areas for improvement and refine your marketing strategies.

Measuring and Analyzing Marketing Efforts for Continuous Improvement

a. Set Measurable Goals: Clearly define your marketing goals and objectives. Whether it's increasing website traffic, generating leads, or closing deals, establish specific and measurable targets. This allows you to track your progress and assess the effectiveness of your marketing efforts.

b. Utilize Analytics Tools: Implement analytics tools, such as Google Analytics or social media analytics, to gather data on user behavior, engagement, and conversions. These insights provide valuable information about the performance of your marketing campaigns and help you make data-driven decisions.

c. Monitor Key Metrics: Regularly monitor key metrics related to your marketing activities. This could include website traffic, conversion rates, engagement on social media platforms, email open rates, or lead generation statistics. By tracking these metrics, you can identify trends, strengths, and areas that need improvement.

d. Conduct A/B Testing: Experiment with different marketing approaches and strategies through A/B testing. Test variations of your messaging, visuals, or calls-to-action to determine what resonates best with your target audience. Analyze the results to optimize your campaigns and improve their effectiveness.

e. Seek Feedback and Reviews: Encourage clients, partners, and industry peers to provide feedback and reviews about their experience working with you. Positive testimonials and reviews can be powerful marketing tools that build trust and credibility. Monitor online platforms and respond to reviews promptly, whether they are positive or negative.

f. Adapt and Evolve: Stay informed about industry trends, market changes, and emerging technologies. Continuously adapt your marketing strategies to stay ahead of the competition and meet the evolving needs of your target audience. Embrace new marketing channels, techniques, and tools that align with your business objectives.

g. Regularly Evaluate and Refine: Conduct regular evaluations of your marketing efforts to assess their impact and ROI. Identify areas that are performing well and those that require improvement. Make data-driven adjustments and refinements to optimize your marketing campaigns for better results.

By continuously measuring and analyzing your marketing efforts, you can identify what's working, make informed decisions, and continuously improve your strategies to attract developers and investors.

CHAPTER 7

INVESTING AND BUILD WEALTH

Tunde firmly believed in practicing what he preached. He understood that investing in the same real estate market he sold would not only diversify his portfolio but also strengthen his understanding of the market dynamics. He embarked on a journey of strategic investments, carefully selecting properties with growth potential and attractive returns.

Tunde leveraged his knowledge of the local market to identify promising investment opportunities. He conducted thorough research, analyzed market trends, and consulted with experts to ensure each investment aligned with his long-term goals. He diversified his portfolio by investing in residential properties, commercial spaces, and even undeveloped land.

As Tunde's investment portfolio grew, so did his wealth and credibility. His success in the investment arena further solidified his reputation as a knowledgeable and trusted developer agent. Clients appreciated his firsthand experience in the market, knowing that he practiced what he preached.

Investing in the real estate market can offer numerous benefits, especially when you sell in the same market. By recognizing the advantages, implementing strategies to identify profitable investment opportunities, managing risk, and diversifying your portfolio, you can build long-term wealth through strategic investment decisions. Let's explore each aspect in detail:

Think Investing in the Market You Sell

There are a lot of agents who sell to others but do not own a property. It is wise that you invest in what you sell. Investing in the real estate market you sell can provide several advantages:

a. Market Knowledge: As a real estate agent, you have valuable insights into local market trends, property values, and growth potential. This knowledge gives you an edge in identifying lucrative investment opportunities and understanding the dynamics of the market.

b. Network and Connections: Your existing network of clients, colleagues, and industry contacts can provide access to off-market deals, partnerships, and potential investment opportunities. Leveraging these connections can help you uncover exclusive deals and gain a competitive advantage.

c. Efficient Decision-Making: Familiarity with the local market allows you to make more informed investment decisions. You can quickly assess the potential returns, market demand, and risks associated with a particular property or location, enabling you to act swiftly when opportunities arise.

Strategies for Identifying Profitable Investment Opportunities

As a property agent, being able to help your clients secure profitable investments will place you as a go-to in your industry. To achieve, consider these:

a. Market Research: Conduct thorough market research to identify emerging trends, areas of growth, and opportunities for investment. Analyze historical data, economic indicators, and demographic information to gain insights into market demand, rental yields, and potential appreciation.

b. Networking and Relationships: Cultivate relationships with local real estate professionals, developers, property owners, and investors. Attend industry events, join networking groups, and engage in conversations to stay informed about potential investment opportunities and off-market deals.

c. Property Analysis: Develop strong analytical skills to evaluate investment properties effectively. Consider factors such as location, property condition, rental potential, cash flow projections, and potential for value appreciation. Conduct due diligence, including property inspections, financial analysis, and market comparables, to make informed investment decisions.d. Stay Updated on Real Estate Listings: Regularly monitor real estate listings, both on the market and off-market, to identify properties with potential investment value. Set up alerts, work with listing agents, and leverage technology platforms to stay informed about new listings and price reductions.

Managing Risk and Diversifying Your Real Estate Portfolio

I believe that you don't want to get entangled in messy issues. This is why you must learn how to manage risks and diversify your portfolio. Pay attention to these:

a. Risk Assessment: Evaluate the potential risks associated with each investment opportunity. Consider factors such as market volatility, economic conditions, property-specific risks, and financing risks. Conduct a thorough risk assessment to make informed decisions and minimize exposure to potential losses.

b. Diversification: Diversify your real estate portfolio by investing in different property types, locations, and investment strategies. This spreads risk across a range of assets, reducing the impact of any single investment's performance on your overall portfolio.

c. Professional Guidance: Consider seeking advice from real estate professionals, financial advisors, and legal experts. They can provide valuable insights, help you assess risk, and ensure compliance with regulatory requirements. Their expertise can guide you in making sound investment decisions.

Building Long-Term Wealth through Strategic Investment Decisions

a. Investment Goals: Define your investment goals, whether they are focused on cash flow, long-term appreciation, or a combination of both. Establish clear objectives that align with your financial aspirations and risk tolerance.

b. Financial Planning: Develop a comprehensive financial plan that includes investment strategies, cash flow projections, and exit strategies. Consider factors such as financing options, taxation, and market cycles. Regularly review and adjust your plan as market conditions and personal circumstances evolve.

c. Long-Term Vision: Adopt a long-term perspective when it comes to real estate investments. Real estate values tend to appreciate over time, and holding properties for the long term allows you to benefit from potential appreciation and income growth. Avoid making impulsive decisions based on short-term market fluctuations, as real estate investments typically yield better returns over a longer time horizon.

d. Cash Flow Management: Properly manage the cash flow from your real estate investments. Ensure that rental income covers expenses such as mortgage payments, property maintenance, and management fees. Maintaining positive cash flow allows you to reinvest profits, service debt, and build wealth over time.

e. Regular Evaluation: Regularly evaluate the performance of your real estate investments. Monitor rental income, property values, vacancy rates, and expenses. Assess the overall profitability of each investment and make adjustments as necessary to maximize returns.

f. Reinvesting Profits: Consider reinvesting profits from successful real estate ventures into new investment opportunities. This can accelerate portfolio growth and help you achieve your long-term financial goals. Reinvesting profits allows you to compound returns and expand your real estate holdings over timc.

g. Continuous Learning: Stay informed about industry trends, market dynamics, and investment strategies. Attend seminars, workshops, and conferences to enhance your knowledge and stay up to date with the latest developments in the real estate market. Learning from successful investors and industry experts can help you make better investment decisions.

In conclusion, investing in the real estate market where you sell can be a powerful wealth-building strategy. Also, remember to stay informed, seek professional guidance when needed, and maintain a long-term vision for your real estate investments. With careful planning and prudent decision-making, real estate investing can provide you with financial security and opportunities for substantial growth.

CHAPTER 8

EMBRACE INNOVATION

Tunde understood the importance of continual learning and staying ahead of industry trends. He encouraged his team members to attend conferences, seminars, and workshops to expand their knowledge and skills. They kept themselves updated with the latest market trends, legal regulations, and technological advancements.

Tunde also sought mentorship and guidance from successful developer agents who had achieved remarkable success in their careers. He formed connections with industry veterans, seeking their advice and insights on overcoming challenges and seizing opportunities. Their wisdom and guidance helped Tunde navigate complex situations and make informed decisions.

Embracing innovation, Tunde and his team adapted to the ever-changing landscape of the real estate industry. They implemented emerging technologies such as virtual reality property tours, online property management platforms, and blockchain-based smart contracts. These innovations improved operational efficiency, enhanced customer experiences, and positioned the agency as a forward-thinking industry leader.

Enhancing your professional development as a developer agent is essential for staying competitive and achieving long-term success in the real estate industry. By prioritizing continual learning, actively participating in industry conferences, seeking mentorship, and embracing innovation, you can upgrade your skills, expand your knowledge, and adapt to industry trends. Let's explore each aspect in detail:

Continual learning and upgrading of skills and knowledge will set you apart and place you as an authority. To achieve this,

    a. Stay Informed: Stay updated with the latest trends, regulations, and market dynamics in the real estate industry. Follow industry publications, subscribe to newsletters, and utilize reputable online resources to access valuable information and insights.

b. Expand Your Knowledge Base: Invest in continuous learning to expand your skill set and knowledge base. Focus on areas such as property development, market analysis, financial modeling, zoning regulations, and project management. Continuously upgrading your skills enables you to offer comprehensive services to your clients.

c. Attend Training and Workshops: Participate in training programs and workshops that focus on real estate development and related topics. These opportunities provide a structured learning environment where you can gain practical insights, acquire new skills, and network with industry professionals.

d. Engage in Online Learning: Take advantage of online courses, webinars, and educational platforms that offer real estate development-related content. These resources provide flexibility in learning, allowing you to access valuable information at your own pace.

e. Attend Real Estate Conferences: Regularly attend real estate conferences and industry events that focus on development, construction, and urban planning. These gatherings provide opportunities to learn from industry experts, gain insights into market trends, and network with key stakeholders.

f. Join Professional Associations: Become a member of professional associations and organizations dedicated to real estate development. These associations often host conferences, seminars, and workshops that offer educational sessions, panel discussions, and networking events. Engaging with peers and industry leaders can foster knowledge exchange and collaboration.

g. Participate in Industry-Specific Workshops: Look for workshops and training programs that focus specifically on real estate development. These workshops cover topics such as project financing, feasibility studies, design trends, and sustainable development practices. Participating in such workshops allows you to gain specialized knowledge and skills.

h. Find a Mentor: Seek out experienced and successful developer agents who can serve as mentors. A mentor can provide guidance, share insights, and offer valuable advice based on their industry experience. Establish a professional relationship with a mentor to benefit from their wisdom and expertise.

i. Learn from Peers and Colleagues: Engage with peers and colleagues in the real estate industry, especially those who have experience in development. Attend networking events, join industry-specific groups, and actively participate in discussions. Learning from their experiences and sharing best practices can help you expand your knowledge and improve your skills.

j. Collaborate on Projects: Seek opportunities to collaborate with successful developer agents on projects or joint ventures. This allows you to learn firsthand from their strategies, decision-making processes, and project management techniques.

Embracing Innovation and Adapting to Industry Trends

You cannot be top of your industry if you don't embrace innovation. Every day, we are presented with new ideas and strategies and it is important we are open to embracing them and adapting to trends. To achieve this, we must:

a. Stay Updated on Technology: Keep abreast of technological advancements in the real estate development sector. Embrace tools and software that can streamline processes, improve efficiency, and enhance project management. Explore innovations in areas such as 3D modeling, virtual reality, project management software, and data analytics.

b. Monitor Market Trends: Continuously monitor market trends and consumer preferences in the real estate industry. Stay informed about emerging development trends, sustainable practices, urban planning initiatives, and changing demographics. Adapting your strategies to align with market demands positions you as a forward-thinking developer agent.

c. Foster a Culture of Innovation: Encourage a culture of innovation within your team and organization. Foster an environment where new ideas are welcomed, and employees are encouraged to explore creative solutions to challenges. Emphasize the importance of staying updated with industry trends and emerging technologies. Provide resources and support for experimenting with innovative approaches to real estate development.

d. Embrace Sustainable Practices: Recognize the growing importance of sustainable development in the real estate industry. Stay informed about green building practices, energy-efficient technologies, and environmentally-friendly design principles. Incorporate sustainable elements into your development projects and educate clients about the benefits of sustainable living.

e. Adapt to Changing Demographics: Stay attuned to demographic shifts and changing market demands. Understand the preferences and needs of different generations, such as millennials, baby boomers, and Gen Z. Adapt your development strategies to cater to these evolving demographics, such as creating mixed-use spaces, incorporating smart home technologies, or designing amenities that align with their lifestyle preferences.

f. Explore New Market Opportunities: Continuously evaluate market trends and identify new opportunities for real estate development. Keep an eye on emerging neighborhoods, urban revitalization initiatives, and areas with potential for growth. By identifying untapped markets and niche segments, you can position yourself as a developer agent who offers unique and profitable opportunities to clients.

g. Embrace Data-driven Decision Making: Leverage data analytics and market research to make informed decisions. Utilize tools and platforms that provide insights into market trends, property valuations, and investment opportunities. By incorporating data-driven decision-making into your strategies, you can mitigate risks and optimize your development projects.

CHAPTER 9

ALWAYS BE A STEP AHEAD

As a developer agent, conducting thorough due diligence and research is crucial when evaluating properties, developers, and service providers to uncover genuine products and services. By being diligent in your investigations, you can identify red flags and avoid fraudulent or subpar offerings.

Running a Property Due Diligence covers areas including:

a. Title and Ownership: Verify the property's ownership and conduct a comprehensive title search to ensure there are no legal disputes or encumbrances that could affect the transaction.

Review property records, deeds, and any relevant legal documents.

b. Physical Inspection: Perform a thorough physical inspection of the property to assess its condition, quality, and potential issues. Look for signs of structural damage, maintenance issues, or any discrepancies between the advertised features and the actual state of the property.

c. Documentation Review: Review all relevant documentation related to the property, including permits, licenses, certificates, and regulatory compliance. Ensure that all necessary approvals are in place and that the property meets the required building codes and regulations.

d. Financial Analysis: Conduct a financial analysis of the property, including evaluating rental income potential, operating expenses, and projected return on investment. Verify the accuracy of financial statements and assess the property's financial viability.

You must also run Developer Due Diligence and this should cover:

a. Reputation and Track Record: Research the developer's reputation and track record in the industry. Review their past projects, completed developments, and customer reviews or testimonials. Look for any indications of delays, quality issues, or unethical practices.

b. Financial Stability: Assess the developer's financial stability and capacity to complete the project. Review their financial statements, creditworthiness, and funding sources. Ensure they have adequate resources and a solid financial foundation to successfully execute the project.

c. Legal Compliance: Verify the developer's compliance with all relevant laws, regulations, and permits. Check if there are any legal disputes, pending litigations, or regulatory violations associated with the developer or their previous projects.

d. Project Viability: Evaluate the feasibility and viability of the proposed project. Analyze market demand, competition, and the developer's marketing and sales strategies. Assess the project's profitability, potential risks, and projected timelines.

Service Provider Due Diligence is very important and it covers areas like:

a. Credentials and Expertise: Assess the qualifications, credentials, and expertise of service providers, such as architects, engineers, contractors, and consultants. Verify their licenses, certifications, and professional memberships. Review their previous work and client references.

b. Contractual Agreements: Review all contractual agreements with service providers, ensuring that the terms and conditions are fair, comprehensive, and protective of your interests. Seek legal advice when necessary to ensure compliance with applicable laws and regulations.

c. Reputation and Performance: Conduct thorough research on service providers to assess their reputation and performance. Seek feedback from previous clients, review their portfolios, and evaluate their ability to meet project requirements within budget and on schedule.

d. Insurance and Liability Coverage: Confirm that service providers have appropriate insurance coverage, including professional liability insurance and workers' compensation. This protects you from potential liabilities arising from their work on the project.

e. Compliance with Safety and Environmental Standards: Ensure that service providers adhere to safety protocols and environmental regulations. Verify their compliance with occupational health and safety standards, environmental impact assessments, and sustainable building practices.

Identifying Red Flags and Fraudulent Offerings is something you must build yourself to spot. Look out for the following:

a. Unusually Low Prices or Promises: Be cautious of properties or projects offered at unusually low prices or with promises of high returns. Such offers may indicate potential fraud or unrealistic expectations.

b. Lack of Transparency: If there is a lack of transparency in the information provided by developers or service providers, it can be a red flag.

Ensure that all necessary documents and details are readily available and accessible.

c. Unverifiable Credentials: If developers or service providers are unable to provide verifiable credentials, such as licenses, certifications, or references, it raises concerns about their legitimacy and expertise. Verify the credentials and independently research their professional background.

d. Poor Communication and Unresponsiveness: If there is a lack of timely and clear communication from developers or service providers, or if they are unresponsive to your inquiries or concerns, it may indicate a lack of professionalism or potential issues with their services.

e. Negative Reputation or Reviews: Research the reputation of developers and service providers by checking online reviews, forums, and industry publications. Negative reviews, complaints, or consistent patterns of poor performance should raise caution and prompt further investigation.

f. Incomplete or Misleading Information: Watch out for incomplete or misleading information provided by developers or service providers. Ensure that all information is accurate, transparent, and aligns with industry standards and regulations.

g. High-pressure Sales Tactics: Beware of developers or service providers who use high-pressure sales tactics or create a sense of urgency to make a decision quickly. Take the time to thoroughly evaluate the offering and make an informed decision based on the facts.

h. Lack of Documentation or Contracts: Be cautious if developers or service providers are reluctant to provide written documentation or contracts outlining the terms and conditions of the transaction. A lack of proper documentation raises concerns about accountability and the protection of your interests.

In summary, conducting thorough due diligence and research as a developer agent is essential to uncover genuine products and services while avoiding fraudulent or subpar offerings. Also, prioritize transparency, communication, and adherence to legal and ethical standards throughout the due diligence process.

CHAPTER 10

MASTERING THE ART OF NEGOTIATION

Mastering the art of negotiation is crucial as a developer agent to ensure you can close deals successfully and secure favorable terms for your clients. Negotiation skills play a vital role in achieving the best outcomes in real estate transactions. Now, let's look at the various levels of Negotiation.

Preparation

a. Understand Client Objectives: Begin by thoroughly understanding your client's objectives and priorities. Clarify their desired outcomes, such as the purchase price, terms, timelines, and any specific conditions they want to include in the deal.

b. Research and Gather Information: Conduct comprehensive research on the property, market conditions, and comparable sales in the area. Gather relevant data and information that can support your negotiation position, such as recent property appraisals, market trends, and any unique selling points.

c. Identify Strengths and Weaknesses: Evaluate the strengths and weaknesses of your client's position as well as the counterparties involved in the negotiation. Identify key leverage points that can be used to your advantage during the negotiation process.

d. Define Your Negotiation Strategy: Develop a clear negotiation strategy based on your client's objectives and the gathered information. Outline your preferred terms, potential concessions, and alternative options to help you navigate the negotiation process effectively.

Effective Communication

a. Active Listening: Practice active listening to understand the other party's concerns, motivations, and objectives. By actively listening, you can identify areas of common ground and potential areas for compromise.

b. Clear and Concise Communication: Clearly articulate your client's position, preferences, and requirements during the negotiation. Present your arguments and proposals in a concise and persuasive manner, focusing on the key benefits and value propositions.

c. Non-Verbal Communication: Pay attention to non-verbal cues, such as body language and facial expressions, during the negotiation process. Be mindful of your own non-verbal communication to convey confidence, openness, and respect.

d. Empathy and Rapport: Build rapport with the other party by demonstrating empathy and understanding. Develop a positive and cooperative atmosphere that fosters trust and collaboration, making it easier to find mutually beneficial solutions.

Negotiation Techniques

a. Win-Win Approach: Strive for a win-win outcome where both parties feel satisfied with the final agreement. Look for opportunities to create value and find mutually beneficial solutions that address the interests of all parties involved.

b. Focus on Interests, Not Positions: Dig deeper to understand the underlying interests of the other party. By focusing on shared interests rather than rigid positions, you can explore creative solutions that satisfy both parties.

c. Trade-offs and Concessions: Be prepared to make reasonable trade-offs and concessions during the negotiation process. Identify areas where you can offer concessions that hold lesser importance to your client while gaining favorable terms in critical areas.

d. Problem-Solving Approach: Approach negotiations as a problem-solving exercise rather than a confrontational battle. Collaborate with the other party to find solutions that address any challenges or concerns, and encourage brainstorming for innovative ideas.

e. Maintain Flexibility: Be flexible and adaptable during negotiations. Recognize that the process may involve multiple rounds of discussions and adjustments. Explore alternative options and be open to creative solutions that meet the needs of both parties.

Closing the Deal

a. Sealing the Agreement: Once all parties have reached a consensus, clearly summarize the agreed-upon terms and conditions. Ensure that all parties are in alignment and that there is a mutual understanding of the final agreement.

b. Documentation and Legal Review: Facilitate the documentation process by providing necessary paperwork, contracts, and agreements. Collaborate with legal professionals to ensure that all legal aspects are reviewed and addressed.

c. Timely Execution: Promptly coordinate the execution of the deal, ensuring that all necessary paperwork is signed and completed in a timely manner. Stay organized and proactive to avoid any delays or potential issues during the closing process.

d. Post-Deal Follow-up: After the deal is closed, maintain open lines of communication with all parties involved. Follow up to ensure that any outstanding obligations or contingencies are fulfilled as agreed upon in the contract. Foster positive relationships by demonstrating your commitment to client satisfaction.

e. Review and Learn: Take the time to reflect on each negotiation experience and identify areas for improvement. Evaluate the effectiveness of your strategies and techniques, and consider seeking feedback from clients and colleagues. Continually refine your negotiation skills through ongoing learning and practice.

Remember, negotiation is a skill that can be honed through experience and continuous learning. By mastering negotiation techniques, you can effectively advocate for your clients' interests and secure favorable terms in real estate transactions. Through careful preparation, effective communication, the application of negotiation techniques, and skillful deal closing, you can achieve successful outcomes and establish a reputation as a trusted and skilled developer agent.

CHAPTER 11

UNDERSTANDING THE FINANCIALS

As a developer agent, understanding the financial aspects of your real estate agency is essential for planning for success and long-term wealth. Effective financial management involves various aspects, including budgeting, forecasting, and managing cash flow. By adopting sound financial practices, you can ensure sustainable growth and maximize profitability.

Budgeting

a. Revenue Projections: Start by analyzing historical data and market trends to project your agency's revenue. Consider factors such as sales commissions, referral fees, and any additional income sources. Set realistic and achievable revenue goals based on your market analysis.

b. Expense Identification: Identify and categorize all expenses associated with running your agency. This includes operational costs, marketing and advertising expenses, office rent, employee salaries, professional fees, technology and software expenses, and other overheads. Be thorough in capturing all expenses to create an accurate budget.

c. Expense Allocation: Allocate funds to different expense categories based on their priority and impact on your agency's growth. Ensure that essential expenses, such as marketing and staff training, receive sufficient allocation. Prioritize expenses that contribute directly to revenue generation and client satisfaction.

d. Monitoring and Adjustments: Continually monitor your actual expenses against your budgeted amounts. Regularly review your budget and make necessary adjustments to align it with your evolving business needs and financial goals.

Financial Forecasting

a. Market Analysis: Stay informed about market trends, economic conditions, and industry forecasts. Analyze factors that can impact your business, such as interest rates, property market fluctuations, regulatory changes, and customer preferences. Use this information to make informed financial forecasts.

b. Sales Projections: Based on your market analysis and historical sales data, project your agency's future sales. Consider factors such as market demand, competition, pricing trends, and the pipeline of potential deals. Set realistic sales targets and adjust them periodically based on market conditions.

c. Expense Forecasts: Forecast your agency's expenses by considering both fixed and variable costs. Account for potential changes in expenses due to factors such as inflation, rent increases, and fluctuations in labor costs. Anticipate future expenses accurately to ensure adequate financial planning.

d. Profitability Analysis: Analyze your agency's profitability by comparing projected revenues against forecasted expenses. Assess the viability of different business strategies and evaluate the financial impact of potential growth initiatives. Use this analysis to make informed decisions about resource allocation and business expansion.

Cash Flow Management

a. Cash Flow Projections: Create cash flow projections to forecast the timing and amount of cash inflows and outflows. Consider factors such as commission payments, rental income, loan repayments, and operating expenses. This will help you anticipate any cash flow gaps and plan accordingly.

b. Accounts Receivable Management: Implement effective accounts receivable management practices to ensure timely collection of payments from clients. Establish clear payment terms, follow up on overdue invoices, and consider incentives for early payments. Monitor your accounts receivable closely to maintain healthy cash flow.

c. Expense Control: Maintain strict control over expenses to avoid unnecessary cash outflows. Regularly review and negotiate contracts with service providers to ensure competitive pricing. Look for opportunities to optimize costs without compromising on quality or service.

d. Reserve Funds: Establish reserve funds to manage unforeseen expenses or cash flow fluctuations. Set aside a portion of your earnings as a contingency fund to provide stability during challenging periods or to seize new business opportunities.

e. Financing Options: Evaluate financing options to support your agency's growth and investment activities. Explore options such as business loans, lines of credit, or partnerships that can provide additional capital when needed. Assess the terms and interest rates carefully to choose the most suitable financing option for your business.

Professional Financial Advice

a. Seek Expertise: Consider consulting with a financial advisor or accountant who can provide expert guidance on financial management. A professional with knowledge and experience in the real estate industry can offer valuable insights and help you make informed financial decisions. They can assist with financial planning, tax strategies, investment analysis, and risk management.

b. Regular Financial Reviews: Schedule regular meetings with your financial advisor to review your agency's financial performance. Discuss any challenges, opportunities, or changes in your business that may impact your financial strategy. This proactive approach will ensure that you stay on track towards your long-term financial goals.

c. Stay Informed: Continuously educate yourself about financial management best practices and stay updated on industry trends and regulations. Attend workshops, seminars, or webinars that focus on financial literacy and real estate finance. This ongoing learning will help you enhance your financial acumen and make more informed decisions.

d. Technology and Tools: Utilize financial management software and tools to streamline your financial processes. There are various software solutions available that can assist with budgeting, forecasting, cash flow management, and expense tracking. These tools can automate repetitive tasks and provide real-time financial insights to support your decision-making.

e. Review and Adjust: Regularly evaluate your financial management strategies and performance. Monitor key financial indicators, such as profitability ratios, return on investment, and cash flow ratios. Analyze the effectiveness of your budgeting and forecasting processes, and make adjustments as necessary to ensure your financial goals are being met.

In conclusion, effective financial management is essential for the success and long-term wealth of a developer agent. When you practice sound financial principles, including budgeting, forecasting, and cash flow management, you can ensure sustainable growth and maximize profitability. Seek professional advice, stay informed about industry trends, and leverage technology to streamline your financial processes.

Regularly review and adjust your financial strategies to align with your business goals and market conditions. With diligent financial management, you can position yourself for success and build a strong foundation for long-term wealth as a developer agent.

CHAPTER 12

LEVERAGE NETWORKS

As a developer agent, leveraging networking opportunities is crucial for expanding your professional circle and driving business growth. Networking allows you to establish connections, build relationships, and create a robust network of industry professionals that can contribute to your success.

Networking provides numerous benefits for developer agents. It enables you to expand your reach, gain industry insights, access new opportunities, and develop mutually beneficial relationships. By connecting with other professionals in the real estate industry, you can tap into their knowledge, expertise, and connections. Networking also allows you to stay updated on market trends, industry developments, and potential investment opportunities.

Attend Industry Events and Conferences. Industry events and conferences are excellent platforms for networking as a developer agent. These gatherings bring together professionals from various sectors of the real estate industry, including developers, investors, brokers, and service providers.

Attend relevant events, such as real estate conferences, seminars, and trade shows, where you can meet like-minded individuals and expand your professional circle. Actively engage in conversations, exchange business cards, and follow up with contacts afterward to foster ongoing relationships.

Join Professional Associations and Organizations. Becoming a member of professional associations and organizations in the real estate industry offers valuable networking opportunities. These groups provide platforms for networking events, educational resources, and industry-specific knowledge sharing.

Join associations that align with your areas of expertise or interest, such as the National Association of Realtors (NAR) or local real estate associations. Actively participate in association activities, attend meetings, join committees, and engage with fellow members to establish connections and build your professional circle.

Utilize Online Networking Platforms. Online networking platforms, such as LinkedIn, offer powerful tools for expanding your professional circle as a developer agent. Create a compelling profile that highlights your expertise, experience, and achievements. Connect with industry professionals, including developers, investors, and other real estate agents.

Engage with relevant content, join industry-specific groups, and participate in discussions to establish yourself as a knowledgeable and valuable resource. Utilize the messaging feature to reach out to contacts and build relationships beyond the virtual space.

Engage in Strategic Partnerships. Develop strategic partnerships with other professionals in the real estate industry to expand your network and access new opportunities. Identify complementary service providers, such as architects, contractors, property managers, and financial advisors, with whom you can collaborate.

Establish mutually beneficial relationships by referring business to one another, sharing resources, and collaborating on projects. These partnerships not only enhance your network but also provide value to your clients by offering comprehensive services and expertise.

Attend Local Business and Community Events. Expanding your professional circle goes beyond industry-specific events. Attend local business and community events where you can connect with professionals from various backgrounds.

These events may include chamber of commerce meetings, charity fundraisers, or business networking groups. Engage in conversations, introduce yourself as a developer agent, and learn about the needs and opportunities within the local community. Building relationships beyond the real estate industry can lead to valuable referrals and new connections.

Follow Up and Nurture Relationships. Networking is not just about making initial connections; it's about building and nurturing relationships over time. Follow up with your contacts after networking events, conferences, or meetings. Send personalized follow-up emails, schedule coffee meetings, or invite them to industry-related social gatherings.

Show genuine interest in their work, listen actively, and provide value whenever possible. Building strong relationships requires consistent effort and maintaining regular communication.

Give Before You Receive. Networking is a two-way street, and it's essential to give before you expect to receive. Offer assistance, share resources, and provide valuable insights to your network. Actively look for ways to support your connections and contribute to their success.

By being generous with your knowledge, expertise, and resources, you establish yourself as a trusted and valuable professional within your network. When you provide value to others, they are more likely to reciprocate and support your goals and objectives.

Be Authentic and Memorable. When networking as a developer agent, it's important to be authentic and memorable. Be yourself and let your unique personality and expertise shine through. Share your passion for real estate, engage in meaningful conversations, and actively listen to others.

Make an effort to remember details about your contacts, such as their interests or professional goals, and follow up on those topics in future interactions. By being genuine and memorable, you increase the likelihood of creating lasting and meaningful connections.

Follow Up and Stay Connected. Networking is an ongoing process, and it's important to follow up and stay connected with your contacts. Regularly touch base with your network through emails, phone calls, or in-person meetings.

Share relevant industry updates, articles, or resources that may be of interest to them. Attend industry events together or organize informal gatherings to maintain and strengthen your relationships. Consistent communication and engagement demonstrate your commitment to fostering meaningful connections.

Be a Connector. One of the most powerful ways to expand your professional circle is by being a connector. Actively look for opportunities to connect people within your network who could benefit from each other's expertise or services.

Introduce professionals who have complementary skills or shared interests. By being a connector and facilitating mutually beneficial connections, you position yourself as a valuable resource and increase your visibility within the industry.

Follow Up on Referrals. When your contacts refer business or opportunities to you, make sure to acknowledge and express your gratitude. Follow up promptly on any referrals you receive, and keep your referrer informed about the progress and outcomes.

This demonstrates your professionalism and appreciation for their support. By treating referrals with the utmost care and attention, you enhance your reputation and encourage others to continue referring business to you.

CHAPTER 13

EMBRACE
TECHNOLOGY

Harnessing technology is essential for real estate agents like yourself to streamline processes, enhance productivity, and stay competitive in the industry. By embracing the right tools and platforms, you can automate tasks, improve communication, and efficiently manage your business operations. Here, we will discuss the importance of harnessing technology and provide an overview of essential tools and software for real estate agents:

Customer Relationship Management (CRM) Software

CRM software is a fundamental tool for real estate agents. It allows you to organize and manage your client database, track leads, and automate follow-ups. With a CRM system, you can capture client information, log interactions, schedule appointments, and set reminders for important tasks. It helps you stay organized, maintain strong client relationships, and optimize your sales and marketing efforts.

Property Management Software

If you deal with rental properties, property management software can streamline your operations. These platforms assist in tasks such as lease management, rent collection, maintenance requests, and tenant communication. They provide centralized platforms to efficiently handle property-related tasks and keep track of key information, ensuring smooth operations and excellent tenant experiences.

Transaction Management Tools

Transaction management tools simplify the complex process of real estate transactions. These platforms enable you to create, manage, and track transaction documents and paperwork electronically. They streamline document sharing and collaboration with clients, other agents, and stakeholders involved in the transaction. Features may include e-signatures, document storage, task tracking, and compliance management, helping you navigate the transaction process efficiently.

Virtual Tour and 3D Visualization Software

Virtual tour and 3D visualization software have become increasingly important in the real estate industry. These tools allow you to create immersive virtual tours, interactive floor plans, and 3D renderings of properties. By offering potential buyers a realistic virtual experience, you can showcase properties remotely, save time on physical showings, and attract a broader range of buyers.

Online Listing Platforms and Websites

Having an online presence is crucial in today's digital age. Utilize online listing platforms and create your own professional website to showcase properties and attract clients. These platforms allow you to upload property information, high-quality photos, videos, and detailed descriptions. They provide a centralized location for potential buyers and investors to explore your listings, inquire about properties, and connect with you directly.

Communication and Collaboration Tools

Efficient communication and collaboration are vital for real estate agents. Utilize tools such as email clients, instant messaging platforms, and video conferencing software to communicate with clients, colleagues, and stakeholders. These tools enable you to stay connected, share important information, and conduct virtual meetings, regardless of geographical limitations.

Market Research and Data Analytics Tools

To stay informed about market trends and make data-driven decisions, leverage market research and data analytics tools. These tools provide access to market reports, sales data, property insights, and demographic information. They help you identify investment opportunities, understand market trends, and provide valuable information to your clients.

Social Media and Digital Marketing Platforms

Social media platforms and digital marketing tools are essential for promoting your real estate business and reaching your target audience. Create professional profiles on platforms such as LinkedIn, Facebook, and Instagram to share property listings, market updates, and industry insights. Utilize digital marketing tools to run targeted advertising campaigns, capture leads, and track marketing performance.

Mobile Apps

Mobile apps designed specifically for real estate agents offer convenience and flexibility. These apps allow you to access important information and perform tasks on the go. From managing contacts and scheduling appointments to accessing property data and conducting property searches, mobile apps enable you to stay productive and responsive while away from your desk.

Security and Data Protection Tools

Protecting sensitive client information and data is crucial. Invest in cybersecurity tools and data protection measures to safeguard your clients' information and ensure compliance with data privacy regulations. Implement firewalls, encryption software, and secure cloud storage solutions to protect against cyber threats. Regularly back up your data and educate yourself on best practices for data security to minimize the risk of data breaches.

Online Learning Platforms

Continual learning and professional development are essential for real estate agents. Online learning platforms provide access to a wide range of courses and resources to enhance your skills and knowledge. Invest in industry-specific courses, webinars, and certifications to stay updated on market trends, industry regulations, and best practices. These platforms allow you to learn at your own pace and expand your expertise.

Project Management Tools

If you handle multiple projects simultaneously, project management tools can help you stay organized and meet deadlines. These tools allow you to create tasks, set priorities, allocate resources, and track progress. They provide transparency and accountability for yourself and your team, ensuring that projects are completed efficiently and successfully.

Document Management and Storage Solutions

Efficient document management and storage are critical for real estate agents who deal with a large volume of paperwork. Cloud-based document management solutions enable you to store, organize, and access important documents securely from anywhere. These platforms offer features such as version control, document sharing, and search capabilities, making it easy to retrieve and manage documents when needed.

Financial and Accounting Software

To manage your finances effectively, consider using financial and accounting software. These tools help you track income and expenses, generate financial reports, and streamline the tax preparation process. They provide insights into your business's financial health and ensure accurate record-keeping for compliance purposes.

Data and Analytics Tools

Data and analytics tools provide valuable insights into your business performance, market trends, and client behavior. They help you track key metrics, analyze data, and make informed decisions. By understanding your business's strengths and weaknesses, you can identify areas for improvement and optimize your strategies.

So you see, harnessing technology is vital for real estate agents to enhance efficiency, productivity, and competitiveness. When you embrace these tools and platforms, you can streamline processes, improve client experiences, and achieve greater success in your real estate business.

CHAPTER 14

ADAPTING TO MARKET TRENDS

Adapting to market trends is crucial for real estate agents like yourself to stay ahead of the curve and maintain continued success. By recognizing and responding to evolving market dynamics and changing consumer demands, you can adjust your business model and strategies to effectively meet the needs of your clients. Here, we will discuss the importance of adapting to market trends and provide strategies for staying ahead:

Stay Informed and Research

To adapt to market trends, it's essential to stay informed about the latest industry developments, economic indicators, and consumer behaviors. Continuously research and monitor local and national real estate markets, paying attention to factors such as supply and demand, pricing trends, demographic shifts, and regulatory changes. Stay updated on industry publications, news sources, and reports to gain insights into emerging market trends and anticipate shifts in consumer preferences.

Understand Changing Consumer Needs

Consumer preferences and needs evolve over time, and it's crucial to understand and adapt to these changes. Engage with your clients, listen to their feedback, and proactively seek their input on what they value most in a real estate transaction. Stay attuned to shifts in lifestyle choices, technological advancements, and environmental concerns that impact buyer and seller decisions. By understanding changing consumer needs, you can tailor your services and marketing strategies to effectively meet their expectations.

Embrace Technology and Digital Transformation

Technology plays a significant role in shaping the real estate industry, and embracing it is key to adapting to market trends. Explore and leverage digital tools, platforms, and innovations that can enhance your operations, improve client experiences, and increase efficiency. Embrace virtual tours, 3D visualizations, online listings, digital marketing, and other technological advancements that align with changing consumer behaviors. By integrating technology into your business model, you can attract tech-savvy clients and stay ahead of competitors.

Diversify Your Services

As market trends shift, consider diversifying your services to cater to evolving client needs. Assess the demand for specialized services such as property management, investment consulting, relocation assistance, or sustainable housing solutions. By expanding your service offerings, you can attract a broader client base and tap into new revenue streams. However, ensure that you have the necessary expertise and resources to deliver these services effectively.

Build Strategic Partnerships

Collaborating with other industry professionals can help you adapt to market trends and expand your reach. Build strategic partnerships with mortgage lenders, home stagers, contractors, interior designers, and other relevant professionals. These partnerships allow you to offer a comprehensive suite of services to your clients and provide added value. Collaborate on marketing initiatives, share market insights, and refer clients to each other to create a mutually beneficial network.

Personalize Your Approach

In an increasingly competitive market, personalization can set you apart from the competition. Tailor your services to individual client preferences, considering their unique circumstances, goals, and preferences. Leverage data and technology to gather insights about your clients and deliver personalized experiences throughout the buying or selling process. By understanding your clients on a deeper level, you can provide customized solutions and foster long-term relationships.

Continual Learning and Professional Development

Adapting to market trends requires a commitment to continual learning and professional development. Stay updated on industry best practices, attend conferences, seminars, and workshops, and engage in networking opportunities. Seek mentorship or coaching from experienced professionals who have successfully navigated changing market conditions. By investing in your own growth, you can stay abreast of industry trends, gain new skills, and adapt your strategies accordingly.

Agility and Flexibility

To adapt to market trends, it's important to cultivate agility and flexibility in your approach. Be open to experimentation and be willing to pivot your strategies when necessary. Monitor the outcomes of your initiatives and be willing to adjust your course based on the feedback and data you receive. Stay nimble in your decision-making process and be willing to adapt your business model, marketing strategies, and service offerings based on market trends and consumer demands.

Customer Feedback and Satisfaction

Regularly seek feedback from your clients to understand their experiences and satisfaction levels. Actively listen to their suggestions, concerns, and preferences. Use their feedback to make improvements and adjustments to your services and processes. By prioritizing customer satisfaction and incorporating their input into your business decisions, you can build stronger relationships, generate positive word-of-mouth, and attract new clients.

Networking and Collaboration

Networking is an invaluable tool for staying ahead of market trends. Engage with industry professionals, attend real estate events, join associations, and participate in online forums to connect with peers, exchange knowledge, and gain insights into emerging trends. Collaborate with other agents or agencies on joint ventures or co-marketing initiatives to leverage each other's expertise and expand your reach in the market.

Continuous Market Analysis and Strategy Review

Regularly analyze and review your market strategies to ensure they align with current trends and consumer demands. Monitor key performance indicators, such as lead generation, conversion rates, and customer satisfaction metrics. Identify areas where adjustments or improvements are needed and implement changes accordingly. Continuously refine your marketing, sales, and operational strategies to stay ahead of the curve and maximize your business's potential.

Forward-Thinking and Innovation

To adapt to market trends, cultivate a forward-thinking mindset and embrace innovation. Stay informed about emerging technologies, industry disruptors, and market innovations. Evaluate how these advancements can be integrated into your business to create a competitive advantage. Embrace new marketing channels, tools, and techniques to reach and engage with your target audience. By staying at the forefront of industry trends and embracing innovation, you can position yourself as a leader in the market.

Adapting to market trends is essential for sustained success as a real estate agent. When you stay informed, you can effectively adapt to market trends and remain ahead of the curve. By embracing these strategies, you will be well-positioned to thrive in a dynamic and evolving real estate market.

CHAPTER 15

SEEK GROWTH AND EXPANSION

Embracing growth and expansion is an exciting endeavor as a developer agent, allowing you to scale your real estate business and create long-term success. When you strategically expand and diversify your operations, you can tap into new markets, attract a broader client base, and increase your revenue streams. Let's discuss comprehensive strategies for embracing growth and expansion:

Assess Your Current Business

Before embarking on any growth initiatives, it's crucial to assess your current business. Evaluate your strengths, weaknesses, and areas of opportunity. Identify what sets you apart from competitors and leverage those unique selling points. Analyze your existing client base, revenue streams, and market reach. Understanding your current position will provide insights into areas where expansion and diversification can be most beneficial.

Market Research and Analysis

Conduct comprehensive market research to identify potential growth opportunities. Explore emerging markets, underserved areas, or niche segments within the real estate industry. Analyze market trends, economic indicators, and demographic data to understand the demand and potential profitability of new markets or services. Market research will help you make informed decisions about the best areas for expansion.

Develop a Growth Strategy

Based on your assessment and market research, develop a growth strategy that aligns with your business goals. Set specific objectives for expansion, such as entering new geographical markets, targeting different buyer segments, or offering additional services. Define the timeline, resources, and key performance indicators (KPIs) to track your progress. A well-defined growth strategy provides a roadmap for your expansion efforts.

Expand Geographically

Consider expanding your business into new geographic locations. Research areas with strong real estate potential, economic growth, and favorable market conditions. Assess factors such as population growth, employment opportunities, infrastructure development, and regulatory environment. Establish partnerships with local professionals, such as real estate agents, contractors, or property managers, who can provide local expertise and support.

Diversify Your Services

Diversification can help you capture new revenue streams and cater to a broader client base. Identify complementary services that align with your core business. For example, you could offer property management, real estate investment consulting, or commercial leasing services. Diversifying your services can help you attract different types of clients and create additional value for existing clients.

Strategic Partnerships and Acquisitions

Consider forming strategic partnerships or acquiring existing businesses to expedite your growth. Collaborate with complementary service providers, such as mortgage brokers, home builders, or interior designers, to offer bundled services and expand your client reach. Acquisitions allow you to enter new markets or leverage established brands and client bases. However, ensure that partnerships and acquisitions align with your business objectives and are financially viable.

Build a High-Performing Team

As you scale your business, it's essential to build a high-performing team that can support your growth. Hire professionals with expertise in target markets or specialized areas. Invest in training and development to enhance their skills and keep them up to date with industry trends. Delegate responsibilities and empower your team members to take ownership of their roles. A strong team will drive operational efficiency and enable you to focus on strategic growth initiatives.

Implement Technology Solutions

Leverage technology to streamline your operations and support your growth. Implement customer relationship management (CRM) software to manage client relationships, track leads, and automate workflows. Adopt transaction management platforms to streamline the buying and selling process. Embrace digital marketing strategies, such as social media advertising or search engine optimization (SEO), to expand your online presence and attract new clients.

Enhance Branding and Marketing

As you expand, ensure that your branding and marketing efforts reflect your growth. Revisit your brand identity, including your logo, website, and marketing materials, to ensure they align with your expanded business scope. Develop comprehensive marketing strategies to promote your expanded services and reach new audiences.

Utilize both traditional and digital marketing channels to maximize your visibility and generate leads. Develop a content marketing strategy to establish yourself as an industry thought leader and provide valuable information to your target audience.

Leverage social media platforms, online advertising, email marketing, and search engine optimization (SEO) techniques to expand your online reach and attract potential clients in your target markets.

Monitor and Evaluate Performance

As you embrace growth and expansion, it's crucial to monitor and evaluate your performance regularly. Establish key performance indicators (KPIs) to measure the success of your growth initiatives. Monitor metrics such as revenue growth, market share, customer satisfaction, and employee productivity. Regularly assess your progress and make adjustments as needed to ensure you stay on track with your growth strategy.

Maintain a Focus on Quality and Customer Satisfaction

While expanding your business, it's important not to compromise on quality and customer satisfaction. Ensure that your expanded operations maintain the same level of service excellence that your clients have come to expect.

Focus on delivering exceptional customer experiences and exceeding client expectations. By maintaining a strong reputation for quality and customer satisfaction, you can attract new clients and foster long-term relationships.

Continual Learning and Adaptation

As you navigate the challenges and opportunities of growth, embrace a mindset of continual learning and adaptation. Stay informed about industry trends, emerging technologies, and evolving consumer preferences. Attend conferences, seminars, and workshops to expand your knowledge and network with industry professionals. Be open to feedback from clients, employees, and industry peers, and use it to refine your strategies and improve your operations.

In conclusion, embracing growth and expansion as a developer agent requires careful planning, market analysis, and strategic decision-making. By exploring new markets, diversifying your services, forming strategic partnerships, building a high-performing team, implementing technology solutions, enhancing your branding and marketing, and continually monitoring and evaluating your performance, you can successfully scale your real estate business. Stay adaptable, focus on quality, and always prioritize customer satisfaction to ensure sustainable growth and long-term success.

CONCLUSION

Do you remember Tunde at the beginning of this book? Tunde is now at a point where he is reflecting on his remarkable journey—the ups and downs, the challenges and triumphs. He realized that his success was not solely about personal achievement but also about leaving a lasting impact on the real estate industry in Nigeria.

Tunde's agency had become a beacon of excellence, integrity, and innovation. They had set a new standard for customer service and professionalism in the developer market. The Landmark Agent's secrets had transformed the lives of many real estate agents who had embraced the lessons and applied them to their own careers.

Tunde felt a deep sense of fulfillment as he looked back on the positive changes he had brought to the real estate industry. He knew that he had made a difference in the lives of his clients, providing them with trustworthy guidance and helping them make sound investment decisions.

Tunde's reputation as the Landmark Agent continued to grow, attracting high-profile developers and clients seeking his expertise. He had become a trusted advisor to major real estate projects, offering valuable insights and assisting in the successful completion of large-scale developments. His input was sought after not only for his knowledge but also for his unwavering commitment to transparency and ethical practices.

Beyond his professional achievements, Tunde remained dedicated to giving back to his community. He initiated programs to educate aspiring real estate agents, providing them with the knowledge and tools they needed to excel in the industry. He mentored young professionals, sharing his experiences and guiding them on their own paths to success.

Tunde's story became an inspiration to many. He was approached by publishers to write a book, chronicling his journey and sharing the secrets he had learned along the way. I have documented his journey in this book.

As Tunde's influence expanded, he was invited to speak at international conferences and share his insights on the Nigerian real estate market. His expertise transcended borders, and he became a respected voice in the global real estate community.

The legacy of the Landmark Agent continued to thrive even as Tunde passed the reins of his agency to the next generation of talented professionals. The agency remained committed to the principles of exceptional customer service, transparency, and innovation that had made them a force to be reckoned with in the industry.

Tunde's impact on the real estate industry in Nigeria was undeniable. His story served as a testament to the power of determination, continuous learning, and ethical practices. Through his journey, he had not only transformed his own career but had also elevated the standards of the developer market, creating a positive ripple effect that would benefit agents, clients, and the industry as a whole for years to come.

And so, the Landmark Agent's story lived on—a tale of perseverance, knowledge, and integrity that would inspire generations of real estate professionals to reach new heights in their own careers and make a lasting impact on the world of real estate.

As a developer agent, you have chosen a dynamic and rewarding path in the real estate industry. The secrets of success in this market lie in your ability to continuously learn, adapt, and embrace opportunities for growth. Stay committed to your goals, build strong relationships, and leverage your expertise and knowledge to create value for your clients and stakeholders.

Remember that success is not achieved overnight. It is the result of consistent effort, perseverance, and a willingness to learn from both successes and failures. Stay focused on your long-term vision and take consistent steps towards achieving it. Celebrate your achievements along the way and use any setbacks as learning opportunities to refine your approach.

In this competitive industry, continuous improvement is key. Embrace ongoing professional development, seek out mentorship, and stay informed about market trends and industry best practices. Leverage technology and innovation to enhance your efficiency and provide exceptional service to your clients.

Above all, maintain your passion for real estate and the developer market. Remember why you entered this industry and let that drive you to reach new heights of success. Stay positive, remain resilient, and have confidence in your abilities. With dedication, perseverance, and a commitment to excellence, you can achieve long-term success as a developer agent.

Believe in yourself, stay motivated, and embrace the opportunities that come your way. Your journey as a developer agent holds immense potential for growth and fulfillment. Embrace the secrets of success, learn from your experiences, and continue to strive for excellence. The future is yours to shape, and with determination and perseverance, you can achieve remarkable results in the developer market.